1st Grade Common Core Math Workbook

Daily Practice Questions & Answers That Help Students Succeed

Copyright©2020 Wizo Learning

All rights reserved. No part of this book may be reproduced or transmitted in any form or by any means, electronic or mechanical, including photocopying, recording, or by any information storage and retrieval system without permission of the publisher, except for the inclusion of brief quotations in a review.

ISBN: 978-1-951806-27-9

FREE BONUS

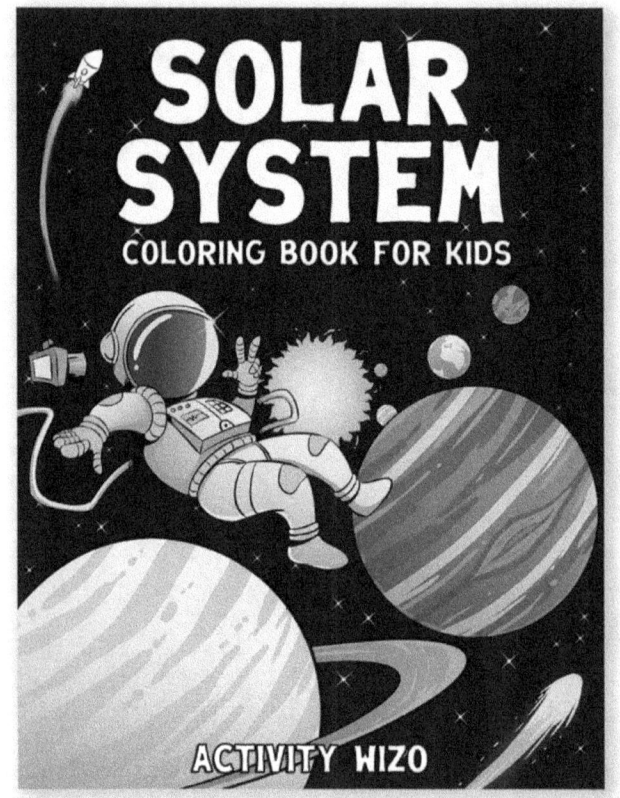

Get This FREE Bonus Now!
Just go to: activitywizo.com/free

Table of Contents

Section 1: Operations and Algebraic Thinking 7

    Counting On 7

    Practicing Addition 9

    Finding the Unknown 12

    Practicing Subtraction 14

    The Equal Sign 17

    The Order of Numbers 19

    The Missing Number 21

    Word Problems 23

Section 2: Numbers and Operations in Base Ten 25

    Count to 120 25

    Reading numbers 29

    Writing Numbers 32

    How Many Do We Have? 33

    Ten Ones 39

    Tens and Ones 42

    Comparing 2 Numbers 44

    Adding 2 Digit Numbers 49

    Finding 10 More or 10 Less 52

    Subtracting Multiples of 10 54

Section 3: Measurement and Data 56

    Comparing Lengths 56

    Measuring Objects 61

    Telling Time By The Hour 63

    Telling Time By The Half Hour 66

    Practice Telling Time 69

    Gathering Data 73

Answer Questions 75

Section 4: Geometry 79
    Sides of Shapes 79
    Identify Shapes 81
    Draw shapes 86
    Dividing shapes 87

Section 5: Mixed Practice 91
    Operations and Algebraic Thinking 91

Answers 103
    Section 1: Operations and Algebraic Thinking 103
    Section 2: Numbers and Operations in Base Ten 112
    Section 3: Measurement and Data 122
    Section 4: Geometry 126
    Section 5: Mixed Practice 129

Section 1: Operations and Algebraic Thinking

<u>Counting On</u>

Have you ever used your fingers to help you add or subtract?

If you have, you have practiced counting on!

When you have trouble adding or subtracting, you can use your counting skills to help you find the answer.

Let's look at an example:

What is 6+4?

To use counting, we can start with 6 and then count on 4.

Hold up 6 fingers. Then, count 4 more, each time you say a number, putting up another finger.

6   7   8   9   10

After counting on 4, you get 10.

So, we know 6+4=10

You can do this with subtraction too!

What is 9-2?

Hold up 9 fingers, then count to 2, putting down a finger each time you say a number.

9   8   7

After counting down 2, you get 7.
So, we know 9-2=7

Let's practice!
Solve each problem using your fingers.

1. 1+6=

2. 6-3=

3. 10-8=

4. 3+1=

5. 5+4=

6. 8-7=

7. 10-2=

8. 4+2=

9. 1+5=

10. 9-3=

11. 7-1=

12. 2+6=

13. 5+3=

Practicing Addition

Let's practice addition! You can use the counting on trick or you can draw pictures to help you solve the problem.

14. 1+4=

15. 5+4=

16. 13+3=

17. 10+8=

18. 18+1=

19. 2+3=

20. 15+2=

21. 4+5=

22. 3+2=

23. 16+1=

24. 11+4=

25. 8+5=

26. 3+5=

27. 19+1=

28. 6+2=

29. 14+3=

30. 5+6=

31. 17+1=

32. 12+1=

33. 4+6=

34. 2+8=

35. 9+7=

36. 7+7=

37. 1+9=

Finding the Unknown

When you complete a subtraction problem, you can think about it as finding the unknown part of an addition problem.

Think about 5-3=

Another way to look at that problem is what number added to 3 will give you 2?

You can count on to find the missing number.

3   4   5

We counted on twice, so 3+2= 5.

That means 5-3=2

Let's practice!

    38. What number added to 7 will give you 10?

    39. What number added to 3 will give you 5?

    40. What number added to 6 will give you 6?

41. What number added to 2 will give you 9?

42. What number added to 7 will give you 9?

43. What number added to 1 will give you 6?

44. What number added to 3 will give you 5?

45. What number added to 4 will give you 8?

46. What number added to 8 will give you 10?

47. What number added to 1 will give you 2?

48. What number added to 2 will give you 4?

49. What number added to 4 will give you 7?

Practicing Subtraction

Let's practice subtraction! You can use the counting down trick, think about it as an addition problem or you can draw pictures to help you solve the problem.

50. 4-1=

51. 20-6=

52. 5-4=

53. 12-4=

54. 19-1=

55. 3-2=

56. 11-3=   57. 18-7=

58. 20-10=   59. 13-2=

60. 17-9=   61. 2-1=

62. 18-8=   63. 6-5=

64. 10-3=   65. 15-11=

66. 7-6=

67. 16-14=

68. 13-2=

69. 9-4=

70. 15-13=

71. 9-5=

72. 8-4=

73. 14-12=

The Equal Sign

In an addition or subtraction problem, the equal sign means the amount on the left side of the problem is the same as the right side of the problem.

Let's look a bit closer.

Look at the problem below represented by shapes.

4   +   4   =   8

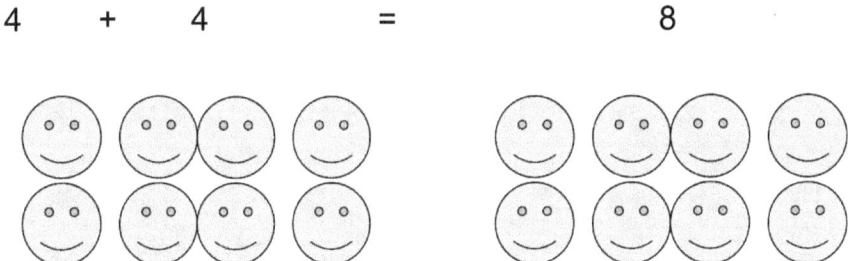

Count the faces. The number of faces on both sides of the equals sign is the same.

If the problem is a subtraction one, you should draw the total number of pictures and cross out an amount. Does the number of pictures left represent the other amount?

Let's practice. Draw pictures to represent each number. Are the sides the same?

74.   3   +   2   =   7

75.   9   -   1   =   8

76.   5   -   3   =   2

77. 4 + 6 = 11
78. 1 + 1 = 2
79. 6 - 4 = 1
80. 12 - 9 = 4
81. 8 + 4 = 11
82. 10 - 6 = 3
83. 2 + 10 = 12
84. 14 - 3 = 9
85. 16 - 2 = 15
86. 3 + 7 = 9
87. 9 + 11 = 20
88. 4 - 3 = 1
89. 11 + 2 = 14
90. 15 - 5 = 10
91. 5 + 1 = 8
92. 13 - 6 = 7
93. 7 + 8 = 15

The Order of Numbers

When you add numbers together, the order in which you add them does not matter.

You can add 5 and 1 as 5+1 or 1+5 and you will still get the same answer.

Try it!

Draw images to represent each problem below.

3 + 2 = 5
2 + 3 = 5

Now count the images do they match? They should!

Let's practice!

94. Which problem is equal to 6+2?
 a. 5+2
 b. 2+2
 c. 8+1
 d. 2+6

95. Which problem is equal to 3+4?
 a. 3+3
 b. 4+3
 c. 4+4
 d. 7+1

96. Which problem is equal to 7+2?
 a. 4+2
 b. 3+8
 c. 2+7
 d. 1+6

97. Which problem is equal to 2+8?
    a. 8+2
    b. 1+7
    c. 2+2
    d. 8+8
98. Which problem is equal to 4+7?
    a. 4+4
    b. 7+4
    c. 7+7
    d. 11+1
99. Which problem is equal to 9+1?
    a. 10+1
    b. 9+2
    c. 1+9
    d. 2+9
100. Which problem is equal to 4+2?
    a. 2+2
    b. 4+4
    c. 2+4
    d. 6+2
101. Which problem is equal to 7+6?
    a. 6+7
    b. 6+6
    c. 7+7
    d. 3+4
102. Which problem is equal to 5+4?
    a. 3+5
    b. 4+4
    c. 5+5
    d. 4+5

103. Which problem is equal to 8+2?
    a. 2+8
    b. 2+2
    c. 8+8
    d. 1+7
104. Which problem is equal to 1+3?
    a. 3+1
    b. 1+1
    c. 3+3
    d. 0+3
105. Which problem is equal to 10+3?
    a. 9+10
    b. 3+3
    c. 3+10
    d. 2+3

The Missing Number

If you are given a missing number, you can use addition OR subtraction to find the missing number.

Let's look at an example.

5+____ = 14

There are two ways to solve this problem.

First, you can subtract 5 from 14 and that will give you the missing amount.

Or, you can ask yourself, how many times must I count up from 5 to reach 14.

Either way, you will get an answer of 9.

Let's practice.

106. 6+____=10

107. ____-6=1

108. 5+3=____

109. 10+____=12

110. ____+1=3

111. ____-2=1

112. 9-____=2

113. 6+5=____

114. 7-____=4

115. ____+8=9

116. 4+____=7

117. ____-4=4

118. ____+2=5

119. 8-____=1

120. ____- 6=3

121. ____+9=11

Word Problems

Now that you have practiced addition and subtraction, you are ready to apply those skills to word problems.

Let's look at an example.

Marcus had 3 books in his backpack. He checked 4 more out from the library. How many books does he now have in all?

First, we need to decide what we know.

We know Marcus started with 3 books.

We also know that he got 4 more books from the library.

Then, we need to decide what we want to know.

We want to know how many books Marcus has in all.

When we are asked how many things in all, that means we have to use addition.

When we are asked how many things are left, that means we have to use subtraction.

To solve, we take the first amount, 3, and then add the second amount, 4.

That gives us a new amount of 7. So we know Marcus now has 7 books.

Let's practice!

122. Alice planted 6 flowers in her garden. One week later, she planted 7 more. How many flowers were now in her garden?

123. Max invited 12 friends to his birthday party. He had 7 friends reply to his invitation. How many friends did not reply?

124. Elizabeth has 8 teddy bears in her collection. She receives 4 more for her birthday. How many bears does she have now?

125. My mom bought 14 apples at the store. She used 9 to make a pie. How many apples are left?

126. You have 6 folders. Your friend has 4 folders. How many more folders do you have than your friend?

127. You see 3 horses at a fence. 4 more come to join them. How many horses are there at the fence in all?

128. You bring 18 cookies to school for the party. You give one to each kid who is present that day. There are 16 kids present. How many cookies do you have left?

129. You are making a rock and mineral collection. You find 8 rocks to add to your collection. You already had 11 rocks. How many rocks are in your collection now?

130. You have 6 pieces of candy. Your mom gives you 4 more pieces. How many pieces do you have in all?

Section 2: Numbers and Operations in Base Ten
Count to 120

Let's begin this section by practicing our counting. Let's first review by counting together to 120.

Point to each number below and count as you point.

1	2	3	4	5	6	7	8	9	10
	11	12	13	14	15	16	17	18	19
	20	21	22	23	24	25	26	27	28
	29	30	31	32	33	34	35	36	37
	38	39	40	41	42	43	44	45	46
	47	48	49	50	51	52	53	54	55
	56	57	58	59	60	61	62	63	64
	65	66	67	68	69	70	71	72	73
	74	75	76	77	78	79	80	81	82
	83	84	85	86	87	88	89	90	91
	92	93	94	95	96	97	98	99	100
	101	102	103	104	105	106	107	108	109
	110	111	112	113	114	115	116	117	118
	119	120							

Now that you have practiced counting, count again but fill in the numbers that are missing.

1	2	3	____	5	6	7	8	____	10
11	12	13	14	15	16	17	18	19	____
____	22	23	24	25	26	27	____	29	
30	31	32	33	34	35	____		37	
____	39	____	____	42	43	44			
45	46	47	48	49	____	51	____		
53	____	55	56	57	58	59	60	61	
62	63	64	____	66	____	68	69		
70	71	72	73	74	____	76	____	78	
79	____	81	____	83	84	85	86	87	
88	89	____	91	92	93	____	95	96	
97	98	99	100	101	____	103	104		
____	106	107	108	109	110	111	112	113	
114	115	116	____	____	119	120			

You can also figure out what number comes next.

What number comes after 12?

One way to find this answer is to count to 12, and see what number comes next. Let's try!

Point to each number and say it out loud.

1 2 3 4 5 6 7 8 9 10 11 12 13

So 13 comes after 12!

Let's practice!

131. What number comes after 23?

132. What number comes after 68?

133. What number comes after 101?

134. What number comes after 90?

135. What number comes after 12?

136. What number comes after 49?

137. What number comes after 72?

138. What number comes after 117?

139. What number comes after 45?

140. What number comes after 78?

141. What number comes after 61?

142. What number comes after 33?

143. What number comes after 80?

144. What number comes after 7?

145. What number comes after 57?

146. What number comes after 103?

147. What number comes after 99?

148. What number comes after 26?

149. What number comes after 84?

150. What number comes after 116?

151. What number comes after 19?

152. What number comes after 54?

153. What number comes after 32?

154. What number comes after 71?

Reading numbers

When we are given numbers, we can read them out loud using words.

Let's look at the words and the numbers they represent:

One	1
Two	2
Three	3
Four	4
Five	5
Six	6
Seven	7
Eight	8
Nine	9
Ten	10
Eleven	11
Twelve	12
Thirteen	13
Fourteen	14
Fifteen	15
Sixteen	16
Seventeen	17
Eighteen	18
Nineteen	19

After 19, words are represented by one word for tens group and then one word for the ones groups.

The ones words are above, the tens words are

Twenty	20
Thirty	30
Forty	40
Fifty	50
Sixty	60
Seventy	70
Eighty	80
Ninety	90

When we get to numbers above 100, we need to add Hundred to represent 100 before the word.

Let's practice.
Write the words each number represents.

155. 34

156. 85

157. 12

158. 108

159. 50

160. 120

161. 78
162. 49
163. 97
164. 63
165. 39
166. 7
167. 100
168. 71
169. 16
170. 26

Writing Numbers

We can take what we learned about words and numbers and use it to write numbers based on words. Let's try it!

Look at the words below. Read them out loud. Write the numbers you say.

Fifty-seven

Do you see 57?

Let's practice!
171. Thirty-nine
172. Seventy-two
173. Ninety-three
174. Sixteen
175. One hundred thirteen
176. Fifty-eight
177. Eighteen
178. Twenty-one
179. Eighty-seven
180. Seventy-eight
181. Five
182. One hundred nine
183. Three
184. Forty-four
185. Twenty-seven
186. Sixty

How Many Do We Have?

When we have a group of objects, we can figure out how many we have by counting the number of objects.

Let's try! Look below and count how many hearts there are.

Point to each heart and say each number as you point.

Did you count 11? You are correct!

You can also draw pictures to represent numbers.

Draw pictures to represent the number 26. You can make simple shapes or smiley faces.

Let's practice!
Count how many we have.

187.

188.

189.

190.

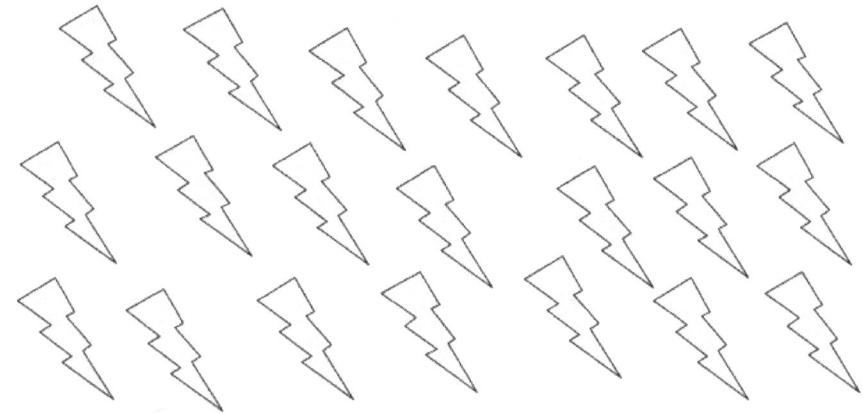

191.

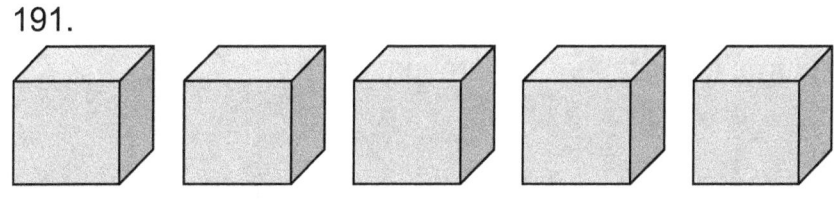

192.

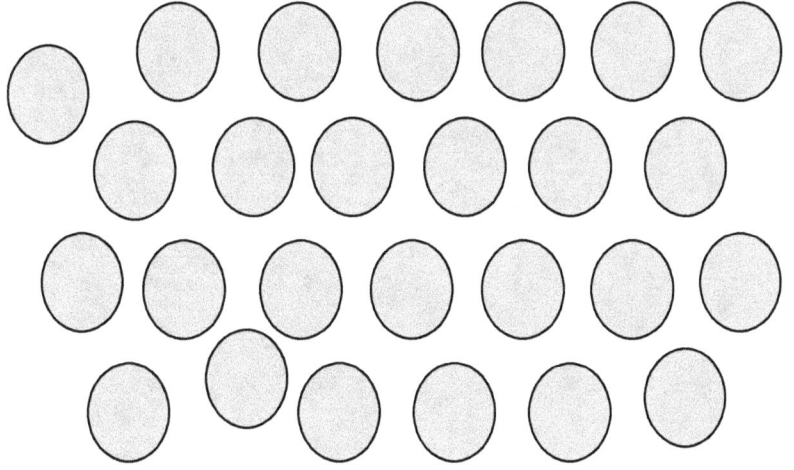

193.

194.

Draw pictures to represent the amount.

195. 12

196. 7

197. 16

198. 9

199. 10

200. 18

201. 1

202. 25

Ten Ones

When we look at a group of 10, it actually represents 10 ones.

Numbers larger than 10 have at least one group of ten and then some ones.

When you are given a group to count, sometimes it is easier to group the tens first and then count the ones.

Let's practice! Group the ones into a set of 10.

203.

204.

205.

206.

207.

208.

209.

210.

Tens and Ones

When we look at 2 digit numbers, the first number is the tens amount and the second number is the ones amount.
Each number tells you the amount of tens and ones.

For example, the number 40, has 4 tens and 0 ones.

Let's practice. Look at the number and tell how many tens and ones are in the number.

211. 60

212. 10

213. 15

214. 40

215. 16

216. 11

217. 80

218. 20

219. 14

220. 9   221. 17

222. 70   223. 90

224. 13   225. 50

226. 30   227. 12

228. 18   229. 19

Comparing 2 Numbers

When we look at 2 numbers, we can decide which one is larger by looking at the ones digit first.

The number with the larger number in the tens digit, will be larger because it has more tens.

The number with the smaller number in the tens digit, will be smaller because it has less tens.

Let's try it.
Which number is larger?   59 or 81?

Let's look at the tens digit first.   59= 5 tens and 81= 8 tens

8 tens is larger than 5 tens so 81 is larger than 59.

Let's practice!
Circle the larger number.

230.   7 or 59   231.   25 or 88

232.   31 or 39   233.   55 or 72

234.   82 or 11   235.   62 or 4

236. 12 or 94

237. 70 or 60

238. 99 or 42

239. 68 or 17

240. 90 or 25

241. 87 or 60

242. 28 or 8

243. 40 or 90

244. 49 or 23   245. 36 or 82

Circle the smaller number.

246. 11 or 6

247. 72 or 23

248. 26 or 81

249. 99 or 42

250. 45 or 61

251. 73 or 17

252. 7 or 56

253. 81 or 90

254. 69 or 94

255. 43 or 17

256. 4 or 72

257. 82 or 80

258. 63 or 35

259. 55 or 28

260. 34 or 64

261. 80 or 9

Adding 2 Digit Numbers

Now that you have practiced place value, you can begin applying these skills in adding 2 digit numbers.

When you add two digit numbers, you start with the ones number and then add the tens number.

If the ones numbers combined give you more than 10, you need to carry a 1 into the tens column.

Let's look at an example:

```
  14
 +18
```

First, add the ones column: 8+4=12

So you place a 2 under the 8 and then carry a 1 above the 1 in 14.

```
   1
  14
 +18
   2
```

Then, you add 1+1+1 and place the answer to the left of the 2.

Your answer becomes 32.

Let's practice!

262. 26+8   263. 72+4

264. 45+9

265. 61+7

266. 14+8

267. 50+1

268. 92+6

269. 36+5

270. 81+7

271. 48+2

272. 25+3

273. 73+9

274. 12+70

275. 31+50

276. 63+20

277. 58+30

278. 45+40

279. 26+40

280. 70+30

281. 84+10

Finding 10 More or 10 Less

We can also use our knowledge of place value to find 10 more or 10 less than a number.

When we find 10 more, we add 1 to the digit in the tens column.

For example, 10 more than 40 is 50.

When we find 10 less, we subtract 1 to the digit in the tens column.

For example, 10 less than 40 is 30.

Let's practice!

282. What is 10 more than 40?   283. What is 10 less than 50?

284. What is 10 less than 70?   285. What is 10 more than 10?

286. What is 10 less than 20?   287. What is 10 less than 60?

288. What is 10 more than 50?   289. What is 10 less than 30?

290. What is 10 more than 20?   291. What is 10 more than 70?

292. What is 10 less than 80?   293. What is 10 more than 30?

294. What is 10 less than 40?   295. What is 10 less than 10?

296. What is 10 more than 60?   297. What is 10 less than 90?

Subtracting Multiples of 10

We can also use our knowledge of place value to subtract multiples of 10 from any number.

Let's look at an example:

56-30=

To solve, we should look at the tens column.

Take 5-3 to get 2 and then the 6 carries along.

The answer becomes 26.
Let's practice!

298. 52-40

299. 17-10

300. 80-60

301. 72-20

302. 21-10

303. 65-50

304. 99-50

305. 34-30

306. 97-60

307. 86-20

308. 75-70

309. 41-20

310. 54-40

311. 92-30

312. 33-10

313. 67-50

Section 3: Measurement and Data

Comparing Lengths

When we want to know how long something is, we can compare its length to other items around it.
Look at your pencil or writing utensil.

Then, look around the room.

What is something longer than your pencil?

What is something shorter than your pencil?

We can look at items to see which are longer or shorter.
Circle the longer line.

314.

_____

_____

315.

_____

_____

316.

_____

_____

317.

_____

_____

318.

_____

_____

Circle the shorter line.
319. _____

_____

320.

_____

_____

321.

_____

_____

322.
_____

_____

323. _____

_____

324.
_____

_____

Draw three lines and circle the longest one.

325.

326.

327.

328.

329.

330.

Draw three lines and circle the shortest one.

331.

332.

333.

334.

335.

336.

Measuring Objects

We can use small objects to measure the length of larger objects. Let's look at an example.
Look at this line.

_____

We can measure it by using smaller units.

_____

We count each smaller unit to see how many units make up the line.

Let's practice! How many units is each line?

337.

_____

338.

_____

339.

340.

341.

342.

343.

344.

345.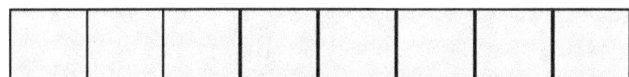

| | | | | | | |

Telling Time By The Hour

When we tell time using a clock, we need to pay attention to the long hand and the short hand.

The short hand is the hour hand. When it is pointing to a number, that is telling us what hour it is.

Look at the clock below. The short hand is pointing to the 3, which tells us that is the hour.

You can write the time like 3:00 or you can say it like Three O'Clock.

Let's practice!
What hour is shown by the clock? Write your answer like 5:00.

346.

347.

348.

349.

350.

351.

352.

353.

354.

355.

Telling Time By The Half Hour

The long hand tells the minutes. In the example, before the long hand was pointing to the 12, which means o'clock.

Each number for minutes means 5 minutes.

The 12 starts us at 0 or o'clock.

Point to each number on the clock face and skip-count by 5.

12 is 0, 1 is 5, 2 is 10, etc.

Stop at 11 and 55.

What number did you get for 6?

You should have gotten 30.

Try again if you didn't.

When the short hand is pointing to 6, it always means 30. We also refer to that as a half hour because 30 minutes is ½ of an hour.

Let's practice.
What time do you see on the clock?

356.

357.

358.

359.

360.

361.

362.

363.

364.

365.

Practice Telling Time
Now let's put it all together and practice telling time. What time is shown on each clock?

366.

367.

368.

369.

370.

371.

372.

373.

374.

375.

376.

377.

378.

379.

380.

381.

382.

383.

384.

385.

386.

387.

388.

Gathering Data

When you complete a survey, you are providing someone information about yourself.

This information is also called data and can be used to examine information about people.

Look at the question below.

How would answer? Circle your favorite pet.

What is your favorite pet?

Dog   Cat
        Fish

When people answer questions, one way we can keep track of their answers is by using tally marks.

To use tally marks, you make a vertical line for each answer 1-4.

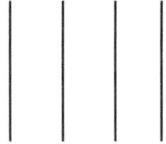

Then, you put a diagonal line to make number 5.

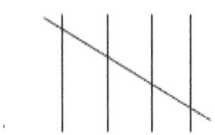

Let's practice!

Count the tally marks and write the correct amounts.

389.

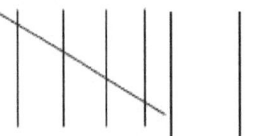

390.

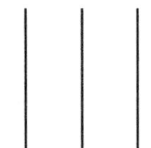

391.

392.

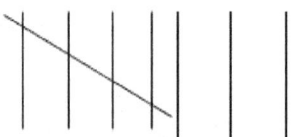

393.

394.

Answer Questions

Once you ask a question and collect answers using tally marks, you can look at your data. You can answer questions such as "how many" and "how many more or less"?

Let's look at an example.
A class was surveyed about their favorite school food.
The results are below.
Pizza:

Hamburgers:

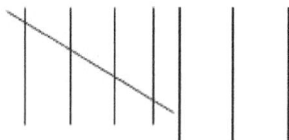

Tacos:

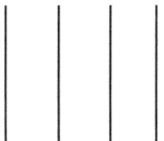

How many students are in the class?

To answer this question, you should count all the tallies. You should have gotten 22.

Let's practice!
Review the data and then answer the questions.

The question was: What is your favorite season?
Summer:

Winter:

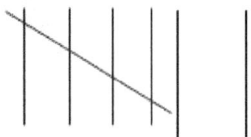

Spring:

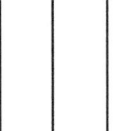

Fall:

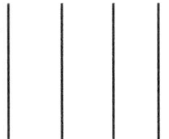

395. How many students were surveyed?

396. How many more students liked summer than fall?

397. How many fewer students liked spring than winter?

398. What was the favorite season?

The question was: How do you get to school?
Walk:

|||| |||| | |
(tally marks: 5 + 5 + 2 = 12)

Ride bus:

|||| |||| |||| ||||
(tally marks: 5 + 5 + 5 + 5 = 20)

Ride in a car:

|||| | |
(tally marks: 5 + 2 = 7)

399. How many students were surveyed?

400. How many more students rode in a bus than in a car?

401. How many students walk to school?

402. How many students ride in a vehicle?

Section 4: Geometry
<u>Sides of Shapes</u>
Can you draw a triangle?

How do you know it is a triangle?

One way that we classify shapes is by the number of sides it has.

A triangle always has 3 sides.

Any shape with three sides is a triangle.

Let's check.
Look at the triangle and count the sides.

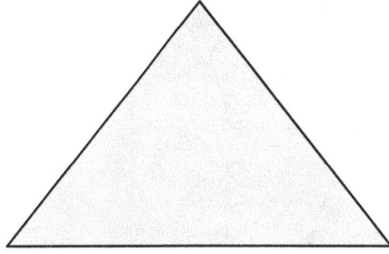

Did you count 3?
Let's practice counting sides! Look at each shape and count the number of sides it has.

403.

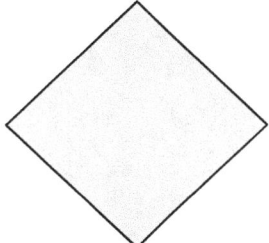

404.

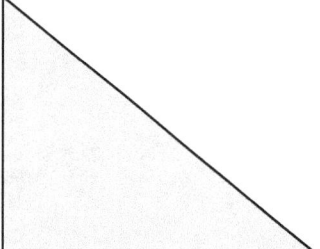

405.

406.

407.

408.

409.

410.

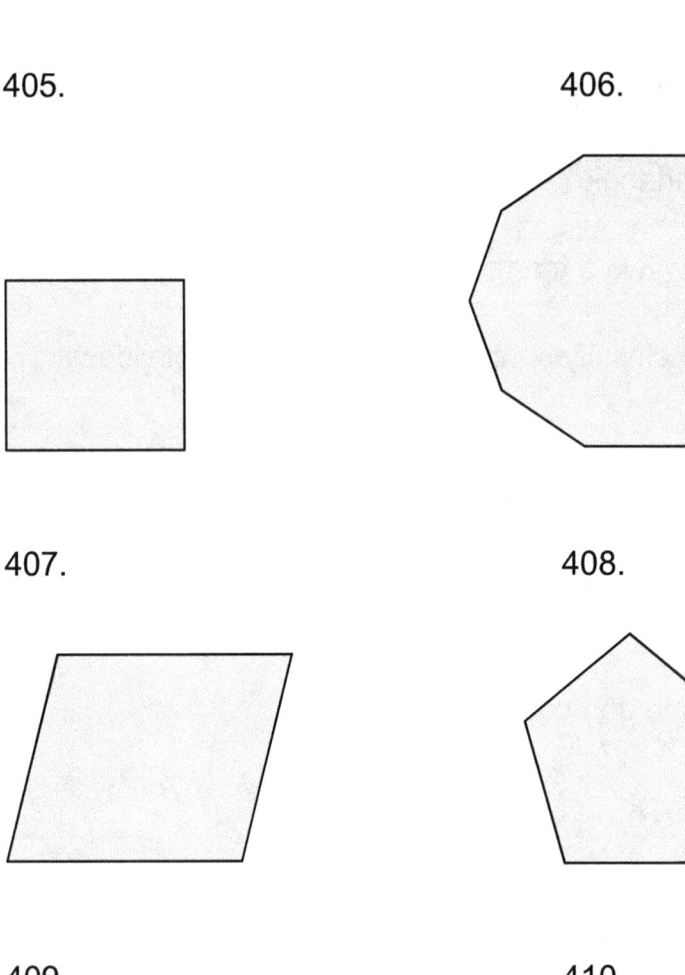

Identify Shapes

We can identify shapes based on the number of sides they have.

It does not matter if a shape is a different size or color, if it has the same number of sides, it is the same shape.

Let's look at an example.

Circle the two squares.

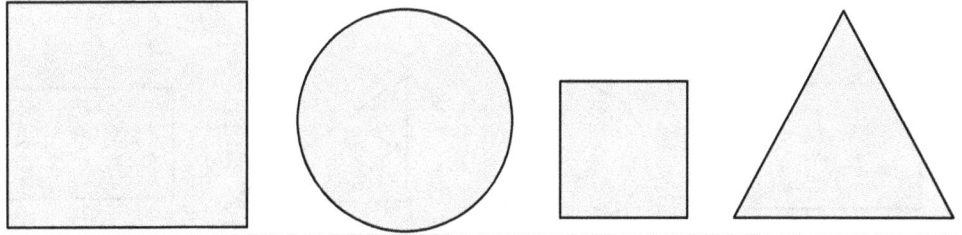

Which two shapes did you circle?

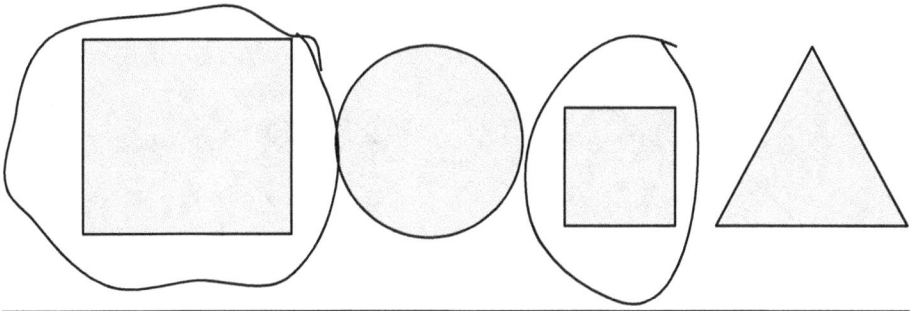

Both of those shapes have four equal sides, so they are both squares.

Let's practice!
Circle the shapes that are the same!

411.

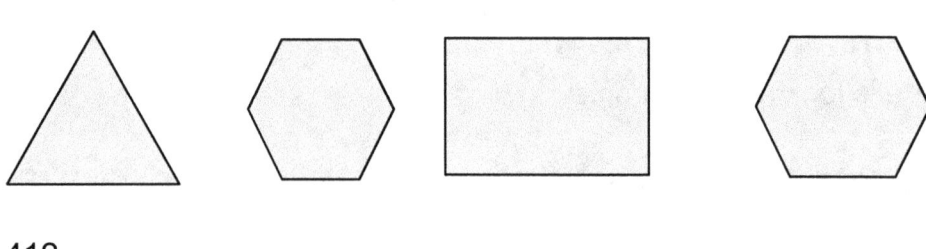

412.

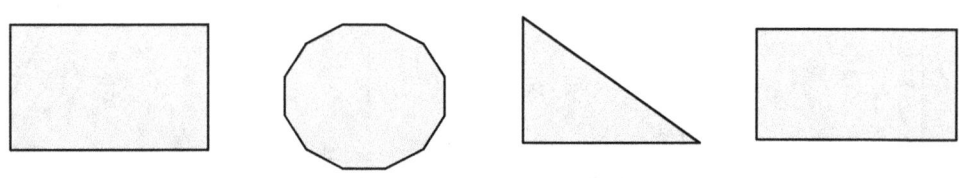

413.

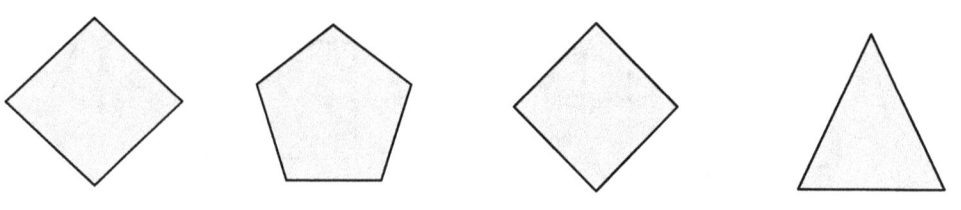

414.

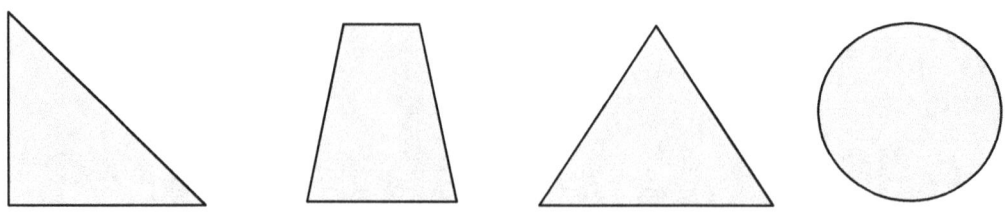

415.

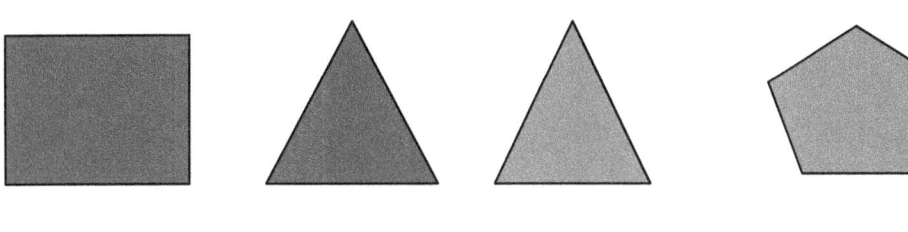

416.

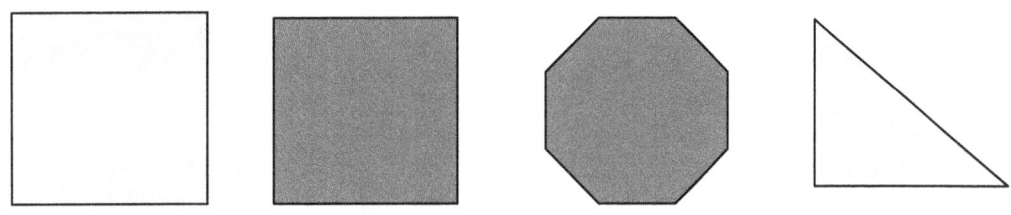

417.

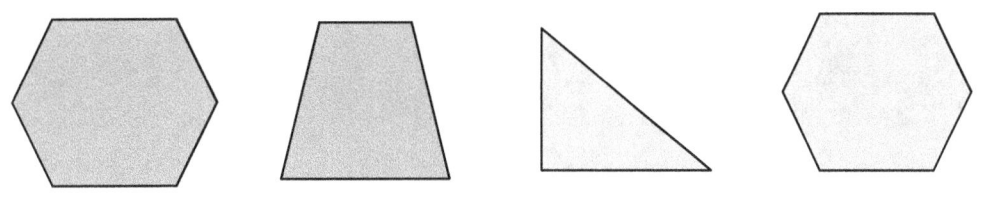

418.

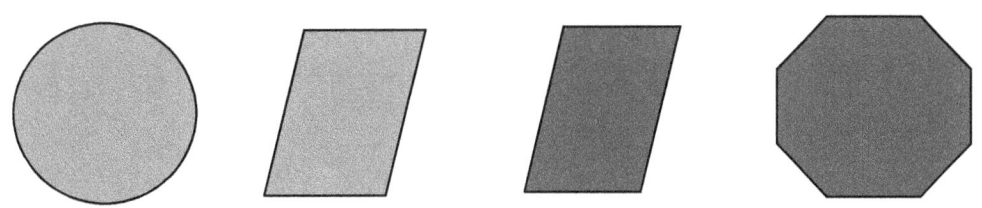

419.

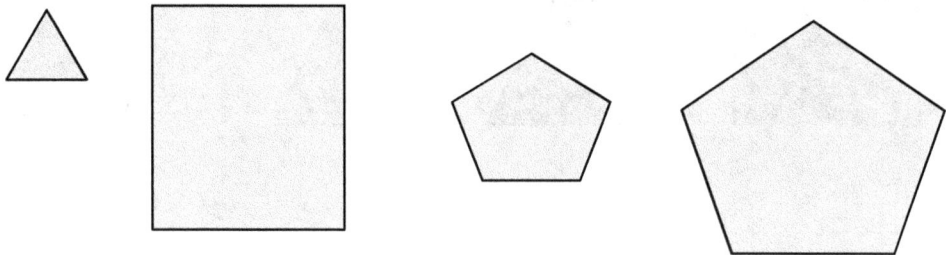

420.

421.

422.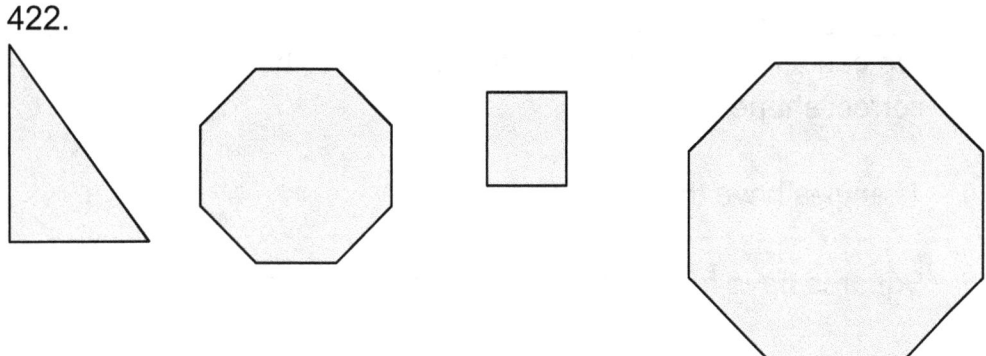

Draw shapes

We can use what we know about shapes to help us draw the correct shape.

Triangles have three sides.

Squares have four sides that are the same size.

Rectangles have four sides, with two sets of matching sizes.

Pentagons have 5 sides.

When you are asked to draw a shape, simply make a figure with that number of sides.

Let's practice!

423. Draw a pentagon.

424. Draw a square.

425. Draw a triangle.

426. Draw a rectangle.

427. Make a shape with at least two other shapes.

428. Make a shape with at least two other shapes.

Dividing shapes

We can divide shapes into smaller equal parts.

We can divide shapes into half or two equal parts.

We can divide shapes into quarter or four equal parts.

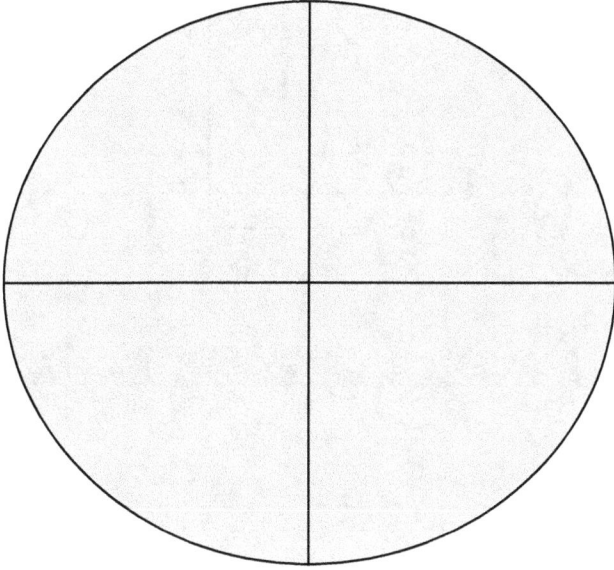

Let's practice!
Divide each shape into 2 equal parts.

429.

430.

431.

432.

Divide each shape into 4 equal parts.

433.

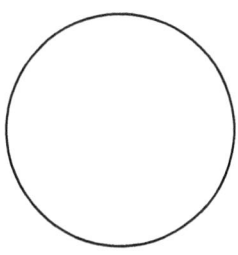

434.

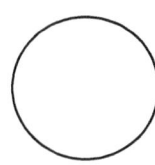

435.

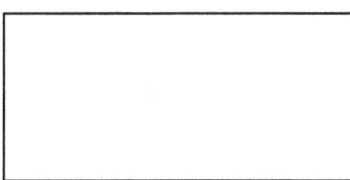

436.

Color the amount given in each problem.

437. Color one half

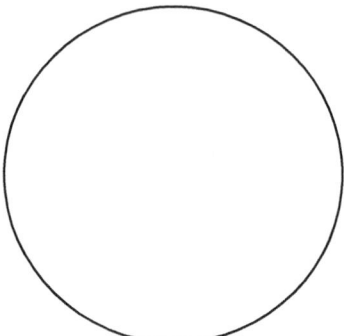

438. Color one quarter

439. Color one fourth one whole

440. Color

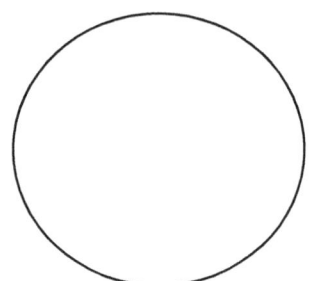

Section 5: Mixed Practice
Operations and Algebraic Thinking

441.   6+5=

442. 8-5=

443.   10-7

444. 2+7=

445. 9+3=

446. 9-2=

447.   6-5=

448. 10+1=

449. 8−1=   450. 4+4=

451. What number added to 6 gives you 8?

452. What number taken from 9 gives you 5?

453. What number added to 2 gives you 7?

454. What number taken from 10 gives you 2?

455. What number taken from 4 gives you 1?

456. _____ + 4 = 10

457. 9 - _____ = 3

458. 5 - _____ = 2

459. Alex's mom made 8 cupcakes. Alex and his 2 brothers each had a cupcake. How many cupcakes were left?

460. Marie's dad collects magnets when they go on vacation. Last month, they went on a trip and he got 4 magnets. This month, he went on a trip and got 8 more magnets. How many magnets did he add to his collection in all?

Numbers and Operations in Base Ten

461.   What number comes after 43?

462.   What number comes after 59?

463.   Write the number 32 in words.

464.   Show the number "seventeen" in numerals.

465.   Write the number "fifty-eight" in numerals.

466. Draw pictures to represent the number 12.

467. How many tens are in the number 61?

468. How many tens are in the number 19?

469. How many ones are in the number 28?

470. How many ones are in the number 30?

471. Circle the larger number: 8 or 16

472. Circle the larger number: 93 or 27

473. Circle the smaller number: 31 or 72

474. Circle the smaller number: 19 or 85

475. 14+37   476. 62+35

477. What is 10 more than 56?

478. What is 10 less than 82?

479. 71-30=   480. 93-50=

Measurement and Data

481.	Circle the longer line.

_____

_____

482.	Circle the shorter line.

_____

_____

483.	Draw three lines and circle the longest.

484.	Draw three lines and circle the shortest.

485. How many units is the line?

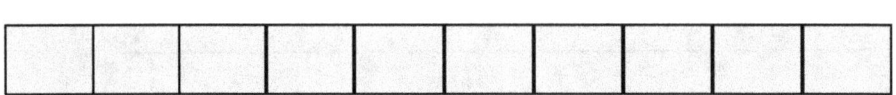

486. Draw 2:00 on a clock.

487. Draw 7:30 on a clock.

A survey was completed on a group of students about their favorite school activity. Use the data gathered below to answer questions 488-490.

The question was: What is your favorite school activity?

Circle Time

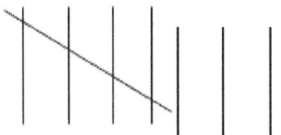

Recess

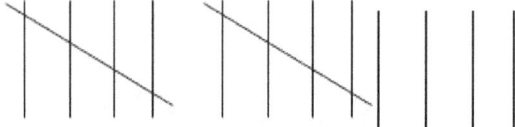

Reading Time

488. How many students enjoy recess the most?

489. How many more students like circle time than reading time?

490. How many students were surveyed in all?

Geometry

491. How many sides does the shape have?

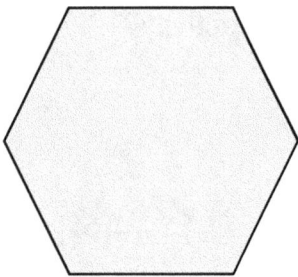

492. How many sides does the shape have?

493. How many sides does the shape have?

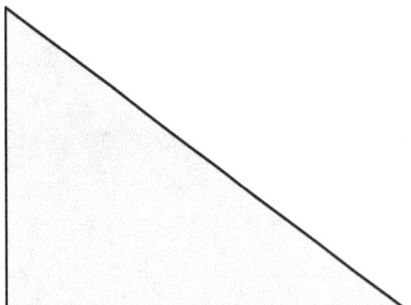

494. Circle the same shape.

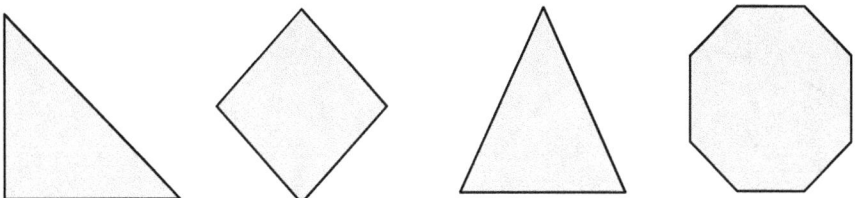

495. Circle the same shape.

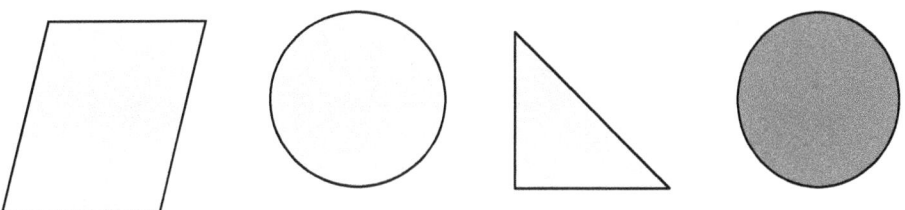

496. Circle the same shape.

497. Draw a triangle.

498. Draw a rectangle.

499.   Divide the circle into 2 parts.

500.   Divide the rectangle into 4 parts.

Answers

Section 1: Operations and Algebraic Thinking

Counting On

1. 7
2. 3
3. 2
4. 4
5. 9
6. 1
7. 8
8. 6
9. 6
10. 6
11. 6
12. 8
13. 8

Practicing Addition
14. 5
15. 9
16. 16
17. 18
18. 19
19. 5
20. 17
21. 9
22. 5
23. 17
24. 15
25. 13
26. 8
27. 20
28. 8
29. 17
30. 11
31. 18
32. 13
33. 10
34. 10
35. 16
36. 14
37. 10

Finding the Unknown
38.3
39.2
40.0
41.7
42.2
43.5
44.2
45.4
46.2
47.1
48.2
49.3

Practicing Subtraction
50. 3
51. 14
52. 1
53. 8
54. 18
55. 1
56. 8
57. 11
58. 10
59. 11
60. 8
61. 1
62. 10
63. 1
64. 7
65. 4
66. 1
67. 2
68. 11
69. 5
70. 2
71. 4
72. 4
73. 2

The Equal Sign

74. Students should draw images that represent each problem. No
75. Students should draw images that represent each problem. Yes
76. Students should draw images that represent each problem. Yes
77. Students should draw images that represent each problem. No
78. Students should draw images that represent each problem. Yes
79. Students should draw images that represent each problem. No
80. Students should draw images that represent each problem. No
81. Students should draw images that represent each problem. No
82. Students should draw images that represent each problem. No
83. Students should draw images that represent each problem. Yes
84. Students should draw images that represent each problem. No
85. Students should draw images that represent each problem. No
86. Students should draw images that represent each problem. No
87. Students should draw images that represent each problem. Yes
88. Students should draw images that represent each problem. Yes
89. Students should draw images that represent each problem. No

90. Students should draw images that represent each problem. Yes
91. Students should draw images that represent each problem. No
92. Students should draw images that represent each problem. Yes
93. Students should draw images that represent each problem. Yes

The Order of Numbers

94. D
95. B
96. C
97. A
98. B
99. C
100. C
101. A
102. D
103. A
104. A
105. C

The Missing Number

106.	4
107.	7
108.	8
109.	2
110.	2
111.	3
112.	7
113.	11
114.	3
115.	1
116.	3
117.	8
118.	3
119.	7
120.	9
121.	2

Word Problems
- 122. 13 flowers
- 123. 5 friends
- 124. 12 bears
- 125. 5 apples
- 126. 2 folders
- 127. 7 horses
- 128. 2 kids
- 129. 19 rocks
- 130. 10 pieces

Section 2: Numbers and Operations in Base Ten
Count to 120
Missing numbers:

1	2	3	4	5	6	7	8	9
10	11	12	13	14	15	16	17	18
19	20	21	22	23	24	25	26	27
28	29	30	31	32	33	34	35	36
37	38	39	40	41	42	43	44	45
46	47	48	49	50	51	52	53	54
55	56	57	58	59	60	61	62	63
64	65	66	67	68	69	70	71	72
73	74	75	76	77	78	79	80	81
82	83	84	85	86	87	88	89	90
91	92	93	94	95	96	97	98	99
100	101	102	103	104	105	106	107	108
109	110	111	112	113	114	115	116	117
118	119	120						

131. 24
132. 69
133. 102
134. 91
135. 13
136. 50
137. 73

138. 118
139. 46
140. 79
141. 62
142. 34
143. 81
144. 8
145. 58
146. 104
147. 100
148. 27
149. 85
150. 117
151. 20
152. 55
153. 33
154. 72

Reading numbers

155. Thirty-four
156. Eighty-five
157. Twelve
158. One hundred eight
159. Fifty
160. One hundred twenty
161. Seventy-eight
162. Forty-nine
163. Ninety-seven
164. Sixty-three
165. Thirty-nine
166. Seven
167. One hundred
168. Seventy-one
169. Sixteen
170. Twenty-six

Writing Numbers

171. 39
172. 72
173. 93
174. 16
175. 113
176. 58
177. 18
178. 21
179. 87
180. 78
181. 5
182. 109
183. 3
184. 44
185. 27
186. 60

How Many Do We Have?
187. 6
188. 9
189. 14
190. 21
191. 5
192. 26
193. 8
194. 3
195. Students should draw the number of pictures that represent the number shown.
196. Students should draw the number of pictures that represent the number shown.
197. Students should draw the number of pictures that represent the number shown.
198. Students should draw the number of pictures that represent the number shown.
199. Students should draw the number of pictures that represent the number shown.
200. Students should draw the number of pictures that represent the number shown.
201. Students should draw the number of pictures that represent the number shown.
202. Students should draw the number of pictures that represent the number shown.

Ten Ones
203. Students should circle 1 group of ten.
204. Students should circle 1 group of ten.
205. There are not enough sticks to circle 1 group of ten.
206. Students should circle 1 group of ten.
207. Students should circle 1 group of ten.
208. Students should circle 1 group of ten.
209. There are not enough sticks to circle 1 group of ten.
210. Students should circle 1 group of ten.

Tens and Ones
211. Six tens
212. One ten
213. One ten five ones
214. Four tens
215. One ten six ones
216. One ten one
217. Eight tens
218. Two tens
219. One ten four ones
220. Nine ones
221. One ten seven ones
222. Seven tens
223. Nine tens
224. One ten three ones
225. Five tens
226. Three tens
227. One ten two ones
228. One ten eight ones
229. One ten nine ones

Comparing 2 Numbers
230. 59
231. 88
232. 39
233. 72
234. 82
235. 62
236. 94
237. 70
238. 99
239. 68
240. 90
241. 87
242. 28
243. 90
244. 49
245. 82
246. 6
247. 23
248. 26
249. 42
250. 45
251. 17
252. 7
253. 81
254. 69
255. 17
256. 4
257. 80
258. 35
259. 28
260. 34
261. 9

Adding 2 Digit Numbers
262. 34
263. 76
264. 54
265. 68
266. 22
267. 51
268. 98
269. 41
270. 88
271. 50
272. 28
273. 82
274. 82
275. 81
276. 83
277. 88
278. 85
279. 66
280. 100
281. 94

Finding 10 More or 10 Less
282. 50
283. 60
284. 60
285. 0
286. 10
287. 50
288. 60
289. 20
290. 30
291. 80
292. 70
293. 40
294. 30
295. 0
296. 70
297. 80

Subtracting Multiples of 10
298. 12
299. 7
300. 20
301. 52
302. 11
303. 15
304. 49
305. 4
306. 37
307. 66
308. 5
309. 21
310. 14
311. 62
312. 23
313. 17

Section 3: Measurement and Data

Comparing Lengths

314. Students should circle the first line.
315. Students should circle the second line.
316. Students should circle the first line.
317. Students should circle the second line.
318. Students should circle the second line.
319. Students should circle the first line.
320. Students should circle the second line.
321. Students should circle the second line.
322. Students should circle the second line.
323. Students should circle the second line.
324. Students should circle the first line.
325. Students should draw 3 lines and circle the one that is the longest.
326. Students should draw 3 lines and circle the one that is the longest.
327. Students should draw 3 lines and circle the one that is the longest.
328. Students should draw 3 lines and circle the one that is the longest.
329. Students should draw 3 lines and circle the one that is the longest.
330. Students should draw 3 lines and circle the one that is the longest.
331. Students should draw 3 lines and circle the one that is the shortest.
332. Students should draw 3 lines and circle the one that is the shortest.
333. Students should draw 3 lines and circle the one that is the shortest.
334. Students should draw 3 lines and circle the one that is the shortest.

335. Students should draw 3 lines and circle the one that is the shortest.

336. Students should draw 3 lines and circle the one that is the shortest.

Measuring Objects
337. 9
338. 5
339. 12
340. 7
341. 4
342. 11
343. 6
344. 2
345. 8

Telling Time By The Hour
(Clocks generated using https://www.helpingwithmath.com/printables/worksheets/time/3md1-clock-face-generator01.htm)

346. 5:00
347. 11:00
348. 2:00
349. 7:00
350. 1:00
351. 10:00
352. 3:00
353. 9:00
354. 4:00
355. 8:00

Telling Time By The Half Hour
356. 8:30
357. 2:30
358. 12:30
359. 1:30
360. 9:30
361. 4:30
362. 5:30
363. 3:30
364. 11:30
365. 7:30

Practice Telling Time
366. 9:00
367. 2:30
368. 3:00
369. 7:00
370. 5:30
371. 5:00
372. 3:30
373. 7:30
374. 1:00
375. 10:00
376. 9:30
377. 11:00
378. 4:00
379. 1:30
380. 8:00
381. 4:30
382. 8:30
383. 2:00
384. 11:30
385. 5:00
386. 12:30
387. 10:30
388. 6:00

Gathering Data
389. 7
390. 3
391. 10
392. 8
393. 2
394. 9

Answer Questions
395. 24
396. 6
397. 4
398. Summer
399. 41
400. 12
401. 13
402. 28

Section 4: Geometry
Sides of Shapes
403. 4
404. 3
405. 4
406. 10
407. 4
408. 5
409. 7
410. 8

Identify Shapes
411. Students should circle the second and fourth shapes.
412. Students should circle the first and fourth shapes.
413. Students should circle the first and third shapes.
414. Students should circle the first and third shapes.
415. Students should circle the second and third shapes.
416. Students should circle the first and second shapes.
417. Students should circle the first and fourth shapes.
418. Students should circle the second and third shapes.
419. Students should circle the third and fourth shapes.
420. Students should circle the second and third shapes.
421. Students should circle the first and third shapes.
422. Students should circle the second and fourth shapes.

Draw shapes
423. Students should draw a shape with 5 sides.
424. Students should draw a shape with 4 equal sides.
425. Students should draw a shape with 3 sides.
426. Students should draw a shape with 4 sides, 2 sets of matching sides.
427. Students should draw a shape made of at least 2 other shapes.
428. Students should draw a shape made of at least 2 other shapes.

Dividing shapes

429. Students should divide the shape into 2 equal parts.
430. Students should divide the shape into 2 equal parts.
431. Students should divide the shape into 2 equal parts.
432. Students should divide the shape into 2 equal parts.
433. Students should divide the shape into 4 equal parts.
434. Students should divide the shape into 4 equal parts.
435. Students should divide the shape into 4 equal parts.
436. Students should divide the shape into 4 equal parts.
437. Students should divide the shape in 2 equal parts and color 1.
438. Students should divide the shape in 4 equal parts and color 1.
429. Students should divide the shape in 4 equal parts and color 1.
440. Students should color the whole shape.

Section 5: Mixed Practice
Operations and Algebraic Thinking
- 441. 11
- 442. 3
- 443. 3
- 444. 9
- 445. 12
- 446. 7
- 447. 1
- 448. 11
- 449. 7
- 450. 8
- 451. 2
- 452. 4
- 453. 5
- 454. 8
- 455. 3
- 456. 6
- 457. 6
- 458. 3
- 459. 5 cupcakes
- 460. 12 magnets

Numbers and Operations in Base Ten
- 461. 44
- 462. 60
- 463. Thirty-two
- 464. 17
- 465. 58
- 466. Students should draw 12 separate objects.
- 467. 6
- 468. 1
- 469. 8
- 470. 0
- 471. 16

472. 93
473. 31
474. 19
475. 51
476. 88
477. 66
478. 72
479. 41
480. 43

Measurement and Data

481. Students should circle the top line.
482. Students should circle the top line.
483. Students should draw three lines and circle the longest.
484. Students should draw three lines and circle the longest.
485. 10 units
486. Students should draw the minute hand pointing to the 12 and the hour hand pointing to 2.
487. Students should draw the minute hand pointing to the 6 and the hour hand pointing to 7.
488. 14
489. 3
490. 27

Geometry
- 491. 6
- 492. 4
- 493. 3
- 494. Students should circle the first and third shape.
- 495. Students should circle the second and last shape.
- 496. Students should circle the first and last shape.
- 497. Students should draw a shape with 3 sides.
- 498. Students should draw a shape with 4 sides, 2 sets of which match.
- 499. Students should divide the circle into 2 equal parts.
- 500. Students should divide the rectangle into 4 equal parts.

www.ingramcontent.com/pod-product-compliance
Lightning Source LLC
Chambersburg PA
CBHW081750100526
44592CB00015B/2362